BEYOND THE MOUND:
Craig Breslow Story

Balancing Baseball Greatness and Intellectual Pursuits

Gregory E. Meyers

Copyright

All right reserved, no part of this publication may be reproduced, distributed or transmitted in any form or by any means, including photocopying, recording or other electronics or mechanical methods without the prior written permission from the publisher except in the case of brief quotations embodied in critical reviews and certern other noncomercial uses permitted by copy right law.

Copyright©Gregory E. Meyers,2023.

Appendix

INTRODUCTION

WHO IS CRAIG BRESLOW

INDIVIDUAL LIFE

EARLY LIFE

HIGH SCHOOL

PROFICIENT VOCATION

POST-PLAYING VOCATION

GROUP ISRAEL

PITCHES

INSIGHT

RAPSODO

GRANTS

GENEROSITY

IN MEDIA

END

INTRODUCTION

In the domain of pro athletics, where speed, strength, and physicality frequently rule, hardly any accounts stand apart like that of Craig Breslow. Past the Hill: The Craig Breslow Story is an enrapturing venture through the duration of a man who accomplished significance on the baseball field and in the domain of mind, an uncommon mix in the realm of sports.

Craig Breslow, a name inseparable from pitching greatness, challenged the cliché form of an expert competitor. He succeeded as a significant association pitcher, yet he likewise embraced an equal way as a devoted researcher. This anecdotal account annals his astounding odyssey, offering bits of knowledge into the difficulties and wins that accompanied adjusting two universes, frequently apparently interestingly.

The baseball field has for quite some time been a venue of legends and legends, where crude ability and coarseness make stars. In any case, Craig Breslow was something other than a star; he was an irregularity. He held a degree from Yale College, a demonstration of his scholarly ability, while likewise holding a spot on the lineup of different Significant Association Ball clubs. This book welcomes you to step onto the hill with him, where curves, change-ups, and fastballs were tossed with accuracy, and off the hill, where the force of schooling was employed with equivalent artfulness.

As we dive into his life, we'll find the penances, the extended periods of training, the scholarly pursuits, and the snapshots of sheer splendor that characterized his vocation. We'll meet the mentors, guides, and partners who propelled and had confidence in him, and we'll investigate the scholastic existence where his commitments reached out a long ways past the field.

Past the Hill: The Craig Breslow Story is a story of persistence, strength, and desire, one that rises above the universe of sports. A story addresses that significance knows no limits, and that genuine legends arise when they rock the boat. Thus, lock in as we set out on this mind boggling venture, investigating the existence of a main vanquished the man hill however wandered past it, offsetting baseball significance with scholarly pursuits such that keeps on motivating every one of us."

WHO IS CRAIG BRESLOW

Craig Andrew Breslow (articulated BREHZ-loh; conceived August 8, 1980) is an American baseball chief and previous expert baseball pitcher. He is right now the Associate Senior supervisor/VP, Overseer of Pitching for the Chicago Fledglings. Breslow played in Significant Association Baseball (MLB) for the San Diego Padres, Boston Red Sox, Cleveland Indians, Minnesota Twins, Oakland Games, Arizona Diamondbacks, and Miami Marlins.

Craig Breslow

Breslow with the Oakland Sports in 2011
Pitcher

Conceived: August 8, 1980 (age 43)

New Asylum, Connecticut, U.S.

Batted: Left

Tossed: Left

MLB debut

July 23, 2005, for the San Diego Padres

Last MLB appearance

September 28, 2017, for the Cleveland Indians

MLB insights

Win-misfortune record

23-30

Procured run normal

3.45

Strikeouts

442

Groups

San Diego Padres (2005)

Boston Red Sox (2006)

Cleveland Indians (2008)

Minnesota Twins (2008-2009)

Oakland Games (2009-2011)

Arizona Diamondbacks (2012)

Boston Red Sox (2012-2015)

Miami Marlins (2016)

Minnesota Twins (2017)

Cleveland Indians (2017)

Vocation features and grants

Worldwide championship champion (2013)

Breslow was chosen in the 26th round of the 2002 MLB draft by the Milwaukee Brewers, and appeared in MLB with the San Diego Padres in 2005. As of the finish of the 2018 season, he positioned fourth among all dynamic left-given MLB pitchers in profession appearances. During his playing vocation, he was recorded at 6 feet 1 inch (1.85 m) and 185 pounds (84 kg).

As a senior at Yale College, where he studied sub-atomic biophysics and natural chemistry, Breslow drove the Elite level with a 2.56 Time. During his MLB profession, he was known as the "most brilliant man in baseball" by columnists at the Minneapolis Star Tribune and The Money Road Diary. In 2010, the Donning News named him the savviest competitor on their best 20 rundown.

INDIVIDUAL LIFE

Breslow put $50,000 in a Boston-based new business that plans bike well disposed business clothing called Service of Supply. The speculation came after his then-life partner, Kelly Shaffer, got him a shirt as a birthday present, Breslow took the shirt out and about and was so satisfied with the exhibition he then purchased two additional shirts and some jeans. Then, at that point, he chose to make the interest in the organization.

Breslow and Shaffer wedded on November 9, 2013 — ten days after he'd won the Worldwide championship with Boston. They have twin young men, Carter and Artisan, brought into the world in June 2015, and girl Livia, conceived December 2018.

EARLY LIFE

Breslow was brought into the world in New Sanctuary, Connecticut, and brought up in Trumbull, Connecticut. He is Jewish, and went to Hebrew school. His family went to Assemblage B'nai Israel in Bridgeport, Connecticut, where he had his Jewish right of passage in 1993. He has abstained while throwing on Yom Kippur, and noted: "Being Jewish is more troublesome in baseball ... yet, I attempt to give my very best regarding focusing on siestas."

Breslow's dad Abe Breslow, an All-American soccer player in school, is an educator and the previous division seat in Actual Training and Wellbeing, and young men tennis trainer and young ladies soccer mentor, at Trumbull Secondary School. His mom, Ann Breslow, is a numerical educator in Bridgeport.

In 1992, when Breslow was 12 years of age, his sister Lesley — two years more seasoned — was determined to have pediatric thyroid disease, for which she had a medical procedure to eliminate every last bit of her thyroid organ (a thyroidectomy). "Something as horrible as that has an enduring effect," Breslow said. "It affirmed my advantage . Being a specialist went from being a lofty calling to something that transforms people." The experience drove Breslow to check out sub-atomic biophysics and natural chemistry. Further down the road, Breslow shaped a non-benefit establishment to assist youngsters with malignant growth.

HIGH SCHOOL

Breslow went to Trumbull Secondary School in Trumbull, Connecticut, graduating in 1998. He was a champion in baseball and soccer, and filled in as group commander in the two games during his senior year.

In baseball, he was the triumphant pitcher in the Class LL State Baseball title game, playing with colleague and future Arizona Diamondbacks second round draft pick and significant association infielder, Jamie D'Antona. He likewise played in youth baseball with future significant association pitcher Charlie Morton. As a senior in secondary school, Breslow played in the

Connecticut/Massachusetts Elite player game at Fenway Park. He was named to the 1998 New Asylum Register All-Region group.

In soccer, he helped lead Trumbull High to their very first state competition triumph. In 1997, he was named to the Fairfield Province Interscholastic Athletic Gathering Young men First-Group Soccer Group. He was known for having an uncanny capacity to score from truly challenging and wide points, and positions among the school's unequaled scorers. Academically he succeeded too, scoring 1420 on his SAT test.

School

Breslow moved on from Yale College in 2002 with a B.A. in atomic biophysics and natural chemistry, and acquired admission to the NYU Institute of Medication, which he conceded.

Breslow was commander of the Yale Bulldogs ball club in the Elite level. As a rookie in 1999, he threw for the Middletown Monsters of the New Britain University Baseball Association; in November 2013 he was enlisted into the NECBL's Lobby of Distinction. As a lesser, he drove Yale with three triumphs and drove the Elite level with a 2.61 procured run normal (Time), striking out 66 players in 51+⅔ innings (positioning thirteenth in the country in strikeouts per nine innings). He procured All-Ivy respects that season, which incorporated a 16-strikeout execution versus Cornell, and a one-hit shutout at Harvard. As a senior, he drove the Elite level with a 2.56 Time.

In 2002, Breslow was named a Jewish Games Survey School Baseball First Group All-American, alongside future significant leaguers Sam Fuld and Adam Greenberg.

Breslow was drafted in the 26th round (769th generally) of the 2002 Significant Association Baseball draft by the Milwaukee Brewers. Breslow conceded acknowledgment to the New York College Institute of Medication in view of his "adoration for the game". As of July 2017, he had conceded his acknowledgment to the clinical school multiple times, as he kept on playing baseball.

Breslow arrived at the significant associations in 2005, the principal Yale graduate to do as such since Ron Dear (1983-95). He pitched his most memorable game for San Diego on July 23, 2005. Breslow was additionally one of six Ivy Leaguers on significant association programs toward the start of the 2009 season. In 2012, Breslow and catcher Ryan Lavarnway turned into the primary Yale graduates to be Significant Association partners starting around 1949, and the principal All-Yale battery in the significant associations beginning around 1883.

PROFICIENT VOCATION

Milwaukee Brewers association (2002-2004)

In 2002, Breslow positioned fifth in the Trailblazer Association with six successes, going 6-2 with a 1.82 Time in 23 appearances out of the pen for the Youngster level Ogden Raptors. He struck out 56 in 54+⅓ innings, and restricted the resistance to a .218 normal. In 2003, he found the middle value of 11+⅓ strikeouts per nine innings for the Single-A Beloit Snappers of the Midwest Association, fanning 80 hitters in 65 innings.

In 2004, Breslow showed up with the Single-A High Desert Free thinkers of the California

Association, going 1-3 with a 7.19 Period. The Brewers delivered Breslow during the 2004 season.

After his delivery, Breslow took the Clinical School Confirmation Test (MCAT) and scored a 34 (the typical score for clinical school candidates was 28), and applied to NYU Clinical School. However the clinical school acknowledged him, they would possibly allow him to begin assuming that he consented to quit playing baseball. "I wasn't prepared to surrender it", he said. "I figured I might still get people out." Beginning around 2013, he was dubious concerning whether after his baseball occupation closes he will go to clinical school, then again become drawn in with the practical side of baseball.

Upper east Association (2004)

Breslow finished the 2004 season throwing for the New Jersey Jackals of the Upper east Association, an autonomous baseball association. He held hitters to a .204 normal and kept 37 strikeouts in 26+⅓ innings, a normal of 12.6 strikeouts per nine innings.

San Diego Padres association (2005)

Endorsed by the San Diego Padres in 2005 for $1 out of a tryout camp, Breslow succeeded, getting $1,500 subsequent to making the Twofold A Southern Association Versatile BayBears, permitting a .212 normal in 52 innings more than 40 excursions while striking out 47 and strolling 17 with a 2.75 Period. He procured his most memorable major association callup on July 23, 2005. He was confused with the group batboy during his most memorable day with the Padres. Breslow turned into the 24th Yalie to play in Significant Association Baseball and the first to arrive at the significant associations since Ron Dear. "It wasn't long after I was playing baseball in the significant affiliations that I figured I could play baseball in the significant affiliations", he said.

Breslow then split the remainder of the time between San Diego and the Triple-A Portland Beavers of the Pacific Coast Association. In 14 help appearances with San Diego, Breslow posted a 2.20

Period without recording a choice. The Padres non-offered Breslow on December 21, 2005.

Boston Red Sox association (2006-2007)

2006

Breslow contributing for the Red Sox 2006.

Breslow marked a small time agreement with the Boston Red Sox on February 1, 2006.

In 2006, Breslow was named a Worldwide Association (Triple-A) Elite player while with the Pawtucket Red Sox. In 67 innings of work for the season, he was 7-1 with a 2.69 Time and struck out a normal of 10.3 hitters per nine innings. He was chosen by his partners as the PawSox Most

Important Pitcher. He was elevated to Boston in the final part of the time, making him the fourth Jewish player (notwithstanding Kevin Youkilis, Gabe Kapler, and Adam Harsh) to play for the Red Sox that year. In 13 help appearances with the Red Sox in 2006, Breslow went 0-2 and posted a 3.75 Period with 12 strikeouts in 12 innings pitched.

Off the field, he assisted Red Sox pitcher With kidding Beckett win a bet against catcher Doug Mirabelli. Breslow determined how frequently a baseball turns when it's tossed 90 miles an hour from the pitcher's hill to home plate. "Josh is curious as to whether I could sort out how often a baseball turns while heading to the plate", Breslow said. "There's a great deal of factors, yet I put in certain figures and concocted deals with a fastball, bend, or slider. It's somewhat basic once you make it happen."

2007

Breslow procured an excursion to the Triple-An Elite player game in July for the subsequent straight season for the Pawtucket Red Sox. Toward the finish of June, Breslow's Period was 1.55. He battled to end the season, completing 2-3 with a 4.06 Period, 25 strolls, 73 strikeouts in 49 help appearances. He was elevated to Boston on September 1, 2007, yet didn't show up and was sent back to Pawtucket on September 2 to make room in the group program for Jon Lester. Breslow was added to the postseason list, and has a ring from winning the 2007 Worldwide championship — without contributing a game the majors that year.

Cleveland Indians (2008)

On Walk 23, 2008, Breslow was asserted off out and out waivers by the Cleveland Indians and was added to the 40-man list. Breslow was out of small time choices, so the Indians needed to keep him on their major association club out of camp, or open him to waivers once more. Breslow won the last right on target the Indians' First day of the season program. "He's solid", Cleveland administrator Eric Wedge said. "I need to have the option to utilize him two innings. That's what he's done — assuming you take a gander at his innings pitched the most recent few years versus appearances."

On May 23, in the wake of contributing seven games and recording a 3.24 Time, Breslow was assigned for task.

Minnesota Twins (2008-2009)

2008

"He's not a person who blows you away on the radar firearm. He's not a major, forcing fellow. However, he gets individuals out. He knows how to pitch and when to toss what. He sorts out ways of getting folks out."

--Twins' associate head supervisor Burglarize Antony

On May 29, 2008, the Minnesota Twins guaranteed Breslow off waivers. In 42 games for the Twins, Breslow went 0-2 with a 1.63 Period, and surrendered just 24 hits in 38+⅔ innings. Lefties hit .183 against him, with a .232 slugging rate, and in save circumstances players batted .100 against him, with a .100 slugging rate. He didn't surrender a spat his last 14 appearances.

Breslow's total 2008 Time of 1.91 in 47 innings was 10th best in the American Class of all pitchers with somewhere around 40 innings pitched, and second-best among AL lefty relievers. He held all hitters to a .191 batting normal, a .265 on-base rate, and a .299 slugging rate.

2009

Playing for the Twins in 2009, Breslow held left-handers to a .211 batting normal and right-handers to a .226 batting normal, yet fought control issues in 17 appearances.

The Twins figured they had a 50-50 possibility losing Breslow when they put him on waivers in May 2009 to clear space on their 25-man program for individual left-hander Sean Henn. Oakland required warm up area help and guaranteed Breslow before his 72-hour waiver period lapsed. Had he cleared, the Twins might have sent him to Significantly increase A Rochester. "We were wanting to keep him", said aide senior supervisor Ransack Antony. "We lost a warm up area fellow without attempting to lose a warm up area fellow", supervisor Ron Gardenhire said. "I sort of got stunned when they told me."

Oakland Games (2009-2011)

2009

Looking for an accomplished left-hander for their warm up area, the Oakland Games guaranteed Breslow off waivers on May 20, 2009. As indicated by collaborator head supervisor David Forst, the A's had attempted to gain him on different events. "I'm amped up for investigating him", A's Director Weave Geren said. "He's a left-given person that is capable. He's had some accomplishment at this level." He was the A's vital lefty out of the warm up area until the end of the time.

Breslow was second in the AL in appearances in 2009, with 77. Players hit as it were .143 against him when there were sprinters in scoring position. He held all players to a .197 batting normal, and a .289 on-base rate.

He likewise kept on intriguing colleagues with his astuteness. "Breslow knows it all", A's left-hander Dallas Braden said. "I genuinely need to be Craig Breslow when I grow up."

2010

Asked in 2010 whether there was a story behind his pullover number, Breslow said: "When you invest energy with numerous associations over 5.5 years, you don't actually tend to think about what number you get."

He was second in the AL in appearances in 2010 for the second year straight, showing up in 75 games (the fifth-most noteworthy single-season complete in A's set of experiences). Just seven of 33 acquired sprinters (21.2%) scored against him, third-best in the AL. He held players to a .194 batting normal, and a .272 on-base rate. Restricting hitters were 0-for-11 with no RBIs against him with the bases stacked, which were the most bases-stacked at bats against an AL pitcher with zero RBIs since the detail was followed start in 1974.

His 71 strikeouts were the most by a lefty reliever in Oakland history, breaking the sign of 69 set by Weave Lacey in 1977. He wrapped up with a vocation high 74+⅔ innings; fourth among American Association relievers. He was named the 2010 Most Important Jewish Pitcher by Jewish Significant Leaguers, as Ryan Braun won hitter respects. Through 2010, he had in his profession permitted just 33 of 151 (21.9%) of acquired sprinters to score, which was the fourth-best rate among pitchers with at least 150 acquired sprinters since the measurement was first followed in 1974. Of his eight vocation MLB saves, five came during the 2010 season.

2011

In 2011, Breslow was 0-2 with a 3.79 Time in 67 games, in which he pitched 59.1 innings. He drove all alleviation pitchers with five pickoffs, and drove American Association relievers with seven found taking.

Arizona Diamondbacks (2012)

On December 9, 2011, Breslow and Trevor Cahill were exchanged to the Arizona Diamondbacks for Ryan Cook, Jarrod Parker, and Collin Cowgill. Since Breslow was the last intervention qualified player for Arizona to be under agreement, he kept away from discretion and an arrangement was made at $1.795 million. His compensation was a $395,000 increment over the 2011 season.

In 40 games and 43+⅓ innings in 2013 for Arizona prior to being exchanged, Breslow had a 2-0 record and a 2.70 Time with 42 strikeouts, and restricted contradicting players to a .233 batting normal. As of the finish of the 2017 season, he was the player with the most innings pitched for Arizona while never losing. He was one of just two pitchers with a 1.000 winning rate with Arizona who had more than one triumph, with the other being Jimmie Sherfy.

Boston Red Sox (2012-2015)

2012

On July 31, 2012, Breslow was exchanged to the Boston Red Sox for outfielder Scott Podsednik and help pitcher Matt Albers. In 23 help appearances with Boston, he was 1-0 with a 2.70 Time and 19 strikeouts. He held rivals to a .206 batting normal, and restricting lefties to a .184 batting normal.

For the season, Breslow was 3-0 with a 2.70 Time in 63 games for Arizona and Boston, and held left-given hitters to a .222 batting normal.

2013

Breslow heating up in the warm up area during the 2013 season

In January 2013, Breslow marked a two-year agreement with the Red Sox for no less than $6.25 million. He got $2.325 million out of 2013, and $3.825 million of every 2014. The Red Sox had a $4 million choice for 2015, with a $100,000 buyout. Breslow started the 2013 season on the handicapped rundown with left shoulder tendinitis. After recovery excursions with Twofold A Portland and Triple A Pawtucket, he was enacted on May 7. He arose as the Red Sox' essential set-up reliever. On September 16, Breslow was named the Red Sox chosen one for the 2013 Roberto Clemente Grant.

In the 2013 ordinary season, Breslow was 5-2 with a 1.81 Time (third among left-gave relievers in the American Association) in 61 games and 59+⅔ innings, and held contradicting players to a .228 batting normal. His 0.65 Period the final part of the time was fourth-best among significant association relievers with somewhere around 25 innings tossed. In his last 28 appearances of the standard season, he permitted just a single run.

In the 2013 American Association Division Series, Breslow pitched 3+⅔ scoreless innings north of three games, indenting a success and permitting two hits and one stroll while striking out four, as the Red Sox crushed Tampa Cove. In the 2013 American Association Title Series, he added 3+⅓ scoreless innings against the Detroit Tigers, bringing his post-season complete to seven scoreless innings in seven appearances, in which he held the resistance to a .130 batting normal. Breslow composed a blog during the 2013 post-season.

During the 2013 end of the season games, he contributed 10 of 16 games, collecting a 2.45 Time.

From 2008 to 2013, Breslow contributed more games (392) than some other left-given reliever other than Matt Thornton, with a 2.82 Time, while restricting hitters to a .224 batting normal.

2014

Breslow started the 2014 season on the impaired rundown, not showing up until the season's tenth game, and gathered a 5.96 Time in 60 appearances for the Red Sox. His presentation stood out pointedly from his 2.82 Period over the earlier six seasons. Breslow saved one game in the 2014 season on August 25, 2014, during an additional inning triumph over AL East adversary Toronto.

The Red Sox declined his $4 million choice, getting him out for $100,000 and making him a free specialist. The Red Sox were still in a situation to re-sign Breslow for less cash. Senior supervisor Ben Cherington said: "He has a ton of good characteristics and we have an incredible connection with him, so we'll see what occurs."

On September 16, Breslow was named the Red Sox candidate for the 2014 Roberto Clemente Grant.

On December 19, the Red Sox re-marked Breslow to a one-year, $2 million agreement.

2015

During the 2015 season, Breslow was 0-4 with one save and a 4.15 Period for Boston in 45 help appearances, striking out 46 and strolling 23 of every 65 innings.

Miami Marlins (2016)

Breslow marked a small time agreement with the Miami Marlins on February 12, 2016, with a significant association choice. Subsequent to going 0-2 with a 4.50 Period in 15 help appearances, he was delivered on July 18, 2016, at his solicitation.

Texas Officers association (2016)

On July 24, 2016, Breslow marked a small time agreement with a quit condition with the Texas Officers. The Officers delivered him on August 7, 2016.

Minnesota Twins second spell (2017)

On February 8, 2017, Breslow marked a small time agreement presented by the Minnesota Twins, which he picked over almost twelve contending offers — some for more cash. He was added to the group's 40-man list on Walk 20, and made the group's first day of the season program toward the month's end. He procured $1.25 million in compensation, and was qualified for $1 million additional conceivable in motivations. His agreement called for him to acquire rewards of

$150,000 at every one of seven unique appearance levels: 40, 45, 50, 55, 60, 65, and 70 games. He was assigned for task on July 24, 2017, in the wake of showing up in 30 games and going 1-1 with a 5.23 Time. He was delivered seven days after the fact.

Cleveland Indians second stretch (2017)

The Cleveland Indians marked Breslow to a small time agreement and relegated him to the Class AAA Columbus Trimmers on August 4, 2017, where he had a 0-0 record with a 3.86 Period in seven help appearances. He was called up to the Indians on August 26, and had a 0-0 record with a 4.15 Time in seven help appearances. He held left-given hitters to a line of .196/.294/.286

throughout the span of the 2017 season. On November 2, he chose for become a free specialist.

Toronto Blue Jays association (2018)

On February 12, 2018, Breslow consented to a small time agreement with the Toronto Blue Jays that incorporated a challenge to spring preparing. He was delivered on Walk 24 in a procedural move, and was re-marked days after the fact to another agreement. On April 2, Breslow consented to go to the Twofold Another Hampshire Fisher Felines in the Eastern Association to keep dealing with his new sidearm conveyance. Generally, he pitched 28.1 innings and was 1-1 with one save and a 5.40 Period in 33 alleviation appearances for the Fisher Felines, the Triple-A Bison Buffaloes in the Worldwide

Association, and the GCL Blue Jays in the Newbie Bay Coast Association.

After the 2018 season, Breslow positioned fourth out of all dynamic left-given MLB pitchers in vocation appearances, with 576. On November 2, 2018, he chose free office.

POST-PLAYING VOCATION

In January 2019, the Chicago Whelps recruited Breslow as their Overseer of Key Drives for Baseball Tasks, joining Theo Epstein in the group's front office. There, he is to "help to assess and carry out information based processes all through all features of Baseball Tasks" and "backing the association's throwing foundation in Player Improvement and the significant associations."

On October 17, 2019, the Whelps elevated Breslow to the place of Overseer of Pitching/Unique Right hand to the President and Head supervisor. His job zeroed in on the essential administration of the club's small time pitching framework to more local effect pitchers.

In November 2020 the Whelps elevated Breslow to the place of Associate Head supervisor/VP, Pitching.

GROUP ISRAEL

Breslow threw for Israel at the 2017 World Baseball Exemplary during the passing round in September 2016. During the initial round of the competition, Breslow was credited with the success in the wake of tossing 26 pitches north of one inning, surrendering two hits and a stroll while recording two strikeouts. Breslow again showed up in the last round of the series, tossing just two pitches while getting one out.

In February 2017, it was declared that Breslow would be on the lineup for Israel at the 2017 World Baseball Exemplary fundamental competition. He pulled out of being in the group in cycle one after the Twins offered him a welcome to spring preparing, and was put in Group Israel's assigned pitcher pool, meaning he could be included later adjusts despite the fact that he didn't play for the group in adjusts a couple.

PITCHES

Breslow's fastball ran at 89 to 92 mph (143 to 148 km/h), and he added a cut fastball during the 80s (roughly 135 km/h) and a sinker. He likewise had an or more overhand curve at 70 to 75 mph (113 to 121 km/h), a normal to better than expected changeup, and a 78 mph (126 km/h) slider/slurve. His capacity to stir up his pitches made him extremely viable. During the 2016 offseason, Breslow dropped his arm space and added a two-crease fastball.

INSIGHT

Breslow was nicknamed the "most astute man in baseball" by Minneapolis Star Tribune Twins beat author La Velle E. Neal III, and The Money Road Diary columnist Jason Turbow expressed: "According to his list of qualifications, Craig Breslow is the savviest man in baseball, in the event that not the whole world." In 2010 the Brandishing News named him the most brilliant competitor on their main 20 rundown. In 2012, Men's Wellness named him one of the Main 10 Savviest Competitors in Elite athletics.

Alluding to the responses he has encountered to the applauses, Breslow said: "There's no limit to the prodding I've taken". Red Sox director John Farrell saw in 2013: "Breslow involves words in a typical discussion that I'm not used to."

With regards to the effect of his knowledge on his baseball execution, Breslow concedes that he dissects video and searches for shortcomings in the "kinematic framework" of his conveyance. Simultaneously, he frequently buys into the "keep it straightforward, moronic" guideline.

RAPSODO

During the 2016 offseason, Breslow started exploring different avenues regarding the Rapsodo Baseball framework to break down his mechanics and twist rate on his throws. His expectation was to work on the development on his pitches and resuscitate his vocation. At the point when he started involving the framework in October 2016, Breslow had 9.45 inches (24.0 cm) of even break on his two-seamer. By January 2017, he had the option to improve and add almost 9 inches (23 cm) of extra development on the two-seamer, bringing about an even break of 18.35 inches (46.6 cm). Vertical development on the pitch likewise expanded by around 6 inches (15 cm).

GRANTS

2005 Southern Association Elite player

2006 Global Association Top pick

2006 SoxProspects.com Elite player

2006 Pawtucket Red Sox Most Important Pitcher

2007 Worldwide Association Elite player

2010 MLB Roberto Clemente Grant Candidate

2010 Oakland Sports Dave Stewart People group Administration Grant Beneficiary

2010 Finalist for the Pen Grant

2010 Trumbull Secondary School Games Lobby of Popularity Inductee

2013 boSox Club Man of the Year

2013 NECBL Corridor of Distinction

2013 MLB Roberto Clemente Grant Candidate

2014 MLB Roberto Clemente Grant Candidate

2014 Recognized Assistance Grant from the Fraternity of Gathering Mishkan Tefila, Chestnut Slope, Massachusetts

GENEROSITY

In 2008, Breslow began the Strike 3 Establishment, a non-benefit good cause that finances pediatric malignant growth research.

The association has collaborated with the Yale-New Asylum Kids' Emergency clinic, Connecticut Youngsters' Clinical Center, Overcome Disease Groundwork of the American Culture of Clinical Oncology, and Kids' Emergency clinic of Philadelphia. The establishment gave $500,000 to the Yale-New Safe house Youngsters' Clinic to assist with improving their Pediatric Bone Marrow Relocate Program.It has additionally made gifts to CureSearch for Kids' Malignant growth,

Connecticut Kids' Clinical Center, Yale's Smilow Disease Emergency clinic, and others.

Breslow desires to hold yearly occasions in Connecticut and during spring preparing. His most memorable advantage raised $100,000, and his second advantage more than $85,000. The foundation has raised more than $3 million.

IN MEDIA

Breslow's university profession and his most memorable year with the Brewers association are to some degree examined in the book Oddball: A Year on the Hill with a Small time Rebel by Matt McCarthy. McCarthy and Breslow were companions and colleagues at Yale, and were in rival Trailblazer Association groups during the 2002 season. He likewise featured in a spoof of Rex Ryan's foot obsession video called "ihaveprettylefthand".

"END

In the pages of Past the Hill: The Craig Breslow Story, we've navigated a remarkable scene of ability, assurance, and keenness. We've followed Craig Breslow's way from the study halls of Yale to the pitcher's hill of Significant Association Baseball, and through each step, he has exemplified the boundless capability of the human soul.

The story of Craig Breslow isn't only the tale of a baseball player; it's a demonstration of the force of self-conviction and the quest for greatness. As we arrive at the finish of this life story, we are helped that the pursuit to remember significance isn't bound to a solitary space. Craig's process embodies that energy knows no limits, and that a promise to one's fantasies can prompt exceptional accomplishments, in any event, when those fantasies exist in isolated universes.

His noteworthy profession, loaded up with exciting triumphs and testing mishaps, fills in as a motivation to all who hope against hope past the customary. It's an update that the quest for information and the quest for athletic greatness are not fundamentally unrelated, yet can coincide and intensify each other.

As we express goodbye to this story, let us convey with us the unyielding soul of Craig Breslow. Allow his story to advise us that in our own lives, we also can endeavor to adjust our interests and our mind, to accomplish greatness both on and off the field.

Craig Breslow's process will keep on rousing people in the future of competitors, researchers, and anybody who has confidence in the capability of the human soul. His story instructs us that we are not restricted by our conditions but rather engaged by our yearnings. Past the hill, past the study hall, and past the limits we see, there lies a universe of vast opportunities for those ready to pursue their fantasies.

Much thanks to you for going along with us on this exceptional excursion. Craig Breslow's story will be for all time a demonstration of the unprecedented levels that can be reached when one thinks for even a second to wander past the common, offsetting baseball significance with scholarly pursuits and making history."

Printed in the USA
CPSIA information can be obtained
at www.ICGtesting.com
CBHW072332021224
18350CB00007B/543